To our families--
our hands holding on for a while
our hearts holding on forever.

Fox Coulee Press
Copyright 2007
All rights reserved.

715-672-4198
www.foxcouleepress.com
letters@foxcouleepress.com
Durand, WI 54736
Published in the USA
ISBN # 978-0-9741199-2-2

HOLDING ON

for
Mothers & Daughters

by Terri Reiland
Illustrated by Gail Pommerening
CD Performed by Vicky Emerson

Best Wishes —
Gail Pommerening

These hands are holding on,
These hands are holding on to my baby...

Once just a dot

of a thought in my womb,

This bit of a blossom

is starting to bloom,

Kicking and hiccupping

and making more room,

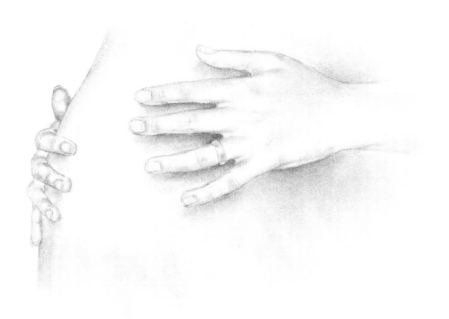

I'm holding on to my baby...

This baby was born

on a wisp of a prayer,

Life filled her lungs

with not a moment to spare,

Now we're cheek to cheek

in this old rocking chair,

I'm holding on to my baby...

She's starting to walk,

we're moving so slow,

She takes her first step,

puts her foot just so,

She plops to her bottom

when I let go,

I'm holding on to my baby...

These hands are holding on,
These hands are holding on to my baby...

Up on my shoulders,

balloon held high,

She squeels at the clowns

when they catch her eye,

And claps to the rhythm band

marching by,

I'm holding on to my baby...

She still feels like

such a tiny tyke,

But she's way too big

for her little trike,

So I'm running and hanging

on the two-wheel bike,

I'm holding on to my baby...

Walking down the grade

school's colorful hall,

With the first day welcome

signs on the wall,

How can I leave her

when she seems so small?

I'm holding on to my baby...

These hands are holding on,
These hands are holding on to my baby...

Sitting on the bench

with her on my knees,

Four hands together

on the piano keys,

Pounding out chopsticks

for hours with ease,

I'm holding on to my baby...

She runs like the wind

in her very first race,

We twirl and howl

when she wins first place,

The joy beaming forth

from her shining face,

I'm holding on to my baby...

We crank up the tunes

and roll up the rug,

And I teach her to dance

the jitterbug,

We collapse and giggle

in a family hug,

I'm holding on to my baby...

These hands are holding on,
These hands are holding on to my baby...

Just yesterday,

she got her license to drive,

Today in a crash,

but she'll survive,

I'm sobbing in thanks

that she's alive,

I'm holding on to my baby...

I'm pinning and poking

the corsage for prom,

And I'm so tickled

to be her mom,

So where's this sadness

coming from?

I'm holding on to my baby...

Pasting up scrapbooks

of each vacation,

And games and sports

and graduation,

Forever photos

of celebration,

I'm holding on to my baby...

These hands are holding on,
These hands are holding on to my baby...

We're packing her bags

and loading her car,

I can't stop a moonbeam

from chasing a star,

I just hope for not too long

and not too far,

I'm holding on to my baby...

Sending her down

the wedding aisle,

Hiding my tears

with a mother's smile,

Can't we stop time

for a little while?

I'm holding on to my baby...

Now it's her turn

for a babe to be born,

I'm thrilled to my bones,

yet a little forlorn

As I rock her baby

from night till morn,

I'm holding on to my baby...

These hands are holding on,

These hands are holding on to my baby...

Together we nurse

her wonderful dad,

Together we mourn,

together so sad,

But heal in the loving

family we've had,

I'm holding on to my baby...

These hands are holding on,
These hands are holding on to my baby...

I've been ill so long;

it's time to let go,

I'm ready, I think,

but wouldn't you know,

The hardest to leave

is this babe I've loved so,

I'm holding on to my baby...

These hands are holding on,

These hands are holding on to my baby...

Now in God's space

I'm cradling her,

With blessings to keep them

all happier,

And to know that

my love is forever,

for sure,

I'm holding on...
I'm holding on...
I'm holding on to my baby...

About the author

In a log home high on a bluff in rural Wisconsin, Terri Reiland writes her books at an old oak table while the light plays over the valley.

As a public health nurse, she is honored to connect with the emotional peaks and valleys of others' lives-- the pregnancies, the births, the deaths, the illnesses, the recoveries. With a family of six, entertainment is home grown in books, music, nature and loved ones. Terri is a also a health columnist and speaker for health seminars.

Also by Terri Reiland:
   Letters from Home
website: www.foxcouleepress.com
email: letters@foxcouleepress.com

About the artist

A self-taught artist, Gail Pommerening expresses her God-given talent in pastel paintings subtly touched with a feeling of soft romance.

Her work is inspired by all things in nature, but Gail is especially fond of the birds and wildlife that reside in the rolling woodlands surrounding her home.

Gail and her family live on a small farm near the scenic town of Plum City, Wisconsin.

Gail's subject versatility has led to nationwide sales of original art and limited edition prints.

website: www.artbygail.com
email: gailkp@centurytel.net

About the musician

Vicky Emerson may have rural roots in Elmwood, Wisconsin, but her music has received national and international acclaim. Touring nationally and releasing five incredibly beautiful albums, has placed Vicky on the map of rising young female artists.

Vicky is currently based in New York City where she continues her career playing shows as well as penning music for TV and film.

website: www.vickyemerson.com
email: vickyemerson@aol.com
CD's from Vicky Emerson
    Reach
    Hold On
    A Winter Moment
    Dream with me
    Moment of Clarity